W9-AVM-232

Strange ... But True?

UFOs

ELIZABETH NOLL

BLACK
RABBIT
BOOKS

Bolt is published by Black Rabbit Books
P.O. Box 3263, Mankato, Minnesota, 56002.
www.blackrabbitbooks.com
Copyright © 2017 Black Rabbit Books

Design and Production by Michael Sellner
Photo Research by Rhonda Milbrett

Library of Congress Control Number: 2015954846

HC ISBN: 978-1-68072-027-3   PB ISBN: 978-1-68072-295-6

Printed in the United States at CG Book Printers,
North Mankato, Minnesota, 56003. PO #1795 4/16

Web addresses included in this book were working and appropriate
at the time of publication. The publisher is not responsible for broken
or changed links.

Contents

CHAPTER 1

What's That in the

A man and his son walked along a river in Florida. Suddenly, they saw a line of lights in the night sky. The lights moved toward them. And they heard a strange noise coming from the lights.

Is It a UFO?

The lights were not stars. They were not planes. They were not **satellites**. What were they? The men thought they might be seeing UFOs.

UFO stands for "**unidentified** flying object." People **claim** to have seen different kinds of UFOs. Many think UFOs are full of aliens. Could that be true?

Flying Saucers

In 1947, a pilot saw nine objects in the sky. He said they moved like **saucers** skipping across water. Since then, people have called UFOs "flying saucers."

CHAPTER 2

Then and Now

People have seen mysterious lights in the sky for thousands of years. Drawings from the 1560s show strange objects in the skies over Europe.

About 100 years ago, people described UFOs that were long and skinny. After 1947, reports of round, silver spaceships became common.

People report new UFO sightings every day. They often describe lights that travel too fast to be planes or stars.

A Crash in Roswell

In 1947, something crashed near Roswell, New Mexico. The U.S. government said it was an Air Force balloon. But about one in five people believe it was really an alien UFO.

CHAPTER 3

Stories

People around the world have UFO stories. Many World War II pilots reported seeing round objects near their planes. The objects looked like fireballs. Pilots called them "foo fighters." No one has been able to explain what the pilots saw.

Former president Jimmy Carter thought he saw a UFO in 1969.

In Alberta, Canada, people built a landing pad for UFOs. So far, only humans have visited it.

Aliens in the Morning

It was 4 a.m. in Lansing, Michigan. A woman named Sherry was sleeping soundly. Suddenly, she jerked awake. Her house was shaking. A bright glow lit up her room. Her skin felt strangely hot. Suddenly, the shaking stopped. The light went out. Did a UFO visit Sherry's house?

UFO HOTSPOTS AROUND THE WORLD

numbers from reports made to MUFON in 2014

467
sightings

CANADA

7,048
sightings

UNITED STATES

56
sightings

MEXICO

41
sightings

BRAZIL

28
sightings

PUERTO RICO

259 sightings
GREAT BRITAIN

27 sightings
GERMANY

63 sightings
SPAIN

167 sightings
INDIA

80 sightings
AUSTRALIA

The Hills

Some people claim aliens took them on board UFOs. Betty and Barney Hill think they were taken. On a road in New Hampshire, they saw a light coming toward them. Then, suddenly, two hours had passed. They couldn't remember what had happened. The Hills believe aliens took them.

ABOUT **10** PERCENT

NUMBER OF AMERICANS WHO SAY THEY HAVE SEEN SPACESHIPS

about 36%
NUMBER OF AMERICANS WHO BELIEVE UFOS ARE REAL

MORE THAN 75%

NUMBER OF AMERICANS WHO THINK IT'S POSSIBLE ALIENS COME TO EARTH

CHAPTER 4

Searching for Answers

Many UFO stories have simple **explanations**. The man and his son who saw a line of lights were mistaken. They were not seeing UFOs. They were looking at ducks. Spotlights **reflected** off the birds' feathers. The strange noise was the ducks' quacking.

Top Seven Things People Mistake for UFOs

#7 LIGHTNING

#6 MISSILE TESTS

#5 CLOUDS

#4 BALLOONS

#3 THE PLANET VENUS

#2 AIRPLANES

#1 MILITARY TESTS

Just a Mistake

Many people mistake ordinary things for UFOs. A weather balloon, a reflection, or blowing dust or snow can sometimes look strange. From 1947 to 1969, the U.S. Air Force **investigated** more than 12,000 UFO reports. They could find no proof that aliens had landed.

Around the world, people report about 192 UFO sightings every day.

Real or Not Real?

History is full of UFO stories.
Believers say the stories prove
something strange is happening.
But others think there's no way
alien spaceships are landing.
What do you think?

Believe It or Not?

Answer the questions below. Then add up your points to see if you believe.

1 **You see a strange light in the sky. What do you think?**

A. Nothing on Earth could make that! (3 points)

B. What is that? (2 points)

C. That must be an airplane or something. (1 point)

2 Are aliens living in outer space?

A. Definitely! (3 points)

B. Maybe. (2 points)

C. No. Scientists would have found them by now. (1 point)

3 Re-read the story of Barney and Betty Hill. What do think?

A. Something strange definitely happened to them. (3 points)

B. Weird. I wonder where those two hours went. (2 points)

C. They probably just fell asleep. (1 point)

. . . .

3 points:
There's no way you think alien UFOs are real.

4–8 points:
Maybe they're real. But then again, maybe they're not.

9 points:
You're a total believer!

claim (KLAYM)—to say that something is true when some people might say it's not true

explanation (ek-splah-NAY-shun)—a statement or fact that explains something

investigate (in-VES-tuh-gayt)—to try to find out the facts

reflect (ree-FLEKT)—light hitting a surface and quickly bouncing off in another direction

satellite (SAT-uh-lyt)—a machine sent to space that moves around the Earth, Moon, Sun, or other planet

saucer (SAW-sur)—a small, round dish to put a cup on

unidentified (un-i-DEN-ti-fyd)—not able to know who someone is or what something is

BOOKS

Higgins, Nadia. *UFOs.* Unexplained Mysteries. Minneapolis: Bellwether Media, Inc., 2014.

Karst, Ken. *Area 51.* Enduring Mysteries. Mankato, MN: Creative Education, 2015.

Perish, Patrick. *Are UFOs Real? Unexplained: What's the Evidence.* Mankato, MN: Amicus, 2014.

WEBSITES

Do Aliens Really Exist?
discoverykids.com/articles/do-aliens-really-exist/

The National UFO Reporting Center
www.nuforc.org

UFO
encyclopedia.kids.net.au/page/uf/UFO

INDEX